100-WHATS
of CREATIVITY

One hundred "What If?" questions to spark your creativity, unmuck your mind, and break through your mental blocks.

By
Don *The Idea Guy* Snyder

100-WHATS of CREATIVITY

For information, contact:

Don The Idea Guy
PO Box 26392
Columbus, OH 43226
614-340-7910

don@100whatsbook.com
www.100whatsbook.com

Dedicated to my Gram,
from her "inventor."

I miss your wisdom,
your meatloaf, and
our Scrabble games.

~D.

CONTENTS

Praise for 100-WHATS

"Don has written an amazing book that will give anyone the creative jolt they need! The creative questions that are packed into this small, practical and stimulating book are a little taste of Don's creative energy – it's like spending a couple of hours with a really smart friend. You will finish this book with many new ideas and want to return to it many times. The only 'what-if' question you don't want to answer is 'what if I never read this book?'"
~ *Kes Sampanthar*
Inventor of ThinkCube
www.MetaMemes.com

"On rare occasions, I actually run across new and creative ways to generate creative ideas --
'100-Whats of Creativity' is one of those gems."
~ *Jamie Nast*
Author of Idea Mapping
www.IdeaMapping.com

"100-WHATS allows you to take the brilliance of Don The Idea Guy with you. Don't miss out on the exponential extra value possible to take your idea to phenomenal success.

This is how the big brains do it!
~ *Jim Canterucci*
Author of Personal Brilliance
www.PersonalBrilliance.com

"Sometimes the best ideas come from examining the possibilities and opportunities we hold in our heads. Don's book is an exercise in unlocking your creative mind by showing how powerful brands and business opportunities can blossom from that one powerful question: 'What If?' What if you didn't read this book? Would your business be as successful as it could be?"
~ *Jim Kukral*
Marketing Ideas Online
www.JimKukral.com

"If your goal is a trip outside the box -- 100-WHATS needs to be your travel agent. Don's quips and questions will help you navigate from 'What Now?' to 'What If?' to 'What the hell am I waiting for!?'"
~ *Chuck Francis*
New Media Consultant
www.Remergemedia.com

"This book is like high-powered, fast-acting creativity juice for non-creative folks, and a great antidote for Adultitis!"
~ *Jason Kotecki*
Cartoonist. Author. Speaker
www.KimAndJason.com

"I read Don's book at 9:00 AM, and by 5:00 PM, I'd already written my next book. That's how powerful it was. That's how much it got me thinking."
~ *Scott Ginsberg*
That Guy with the Nametag
www.HelloMyNameIsScott.com

"The innovation and ideation process is one that requires new and different ways of thinking. Sometimes when you're immersed in a process or overly familiar with a product it's hard to think of new ways in which to probe the issue creatively. That's where we have found the '100-What's of Creativity' to be an invaluable tool. It prompts the user to look at the issue, process, or product in ways that frequently lead to breakthrough ideas, all by simply asking various 'what if' questions. The creativity that results is simply astounding."
~ *Keith Pryor*
Organizational Development Manager
Packaged Food Company

Original Foreword
by Bonnie Neubauer

Great! Great! Great!
And what phenomenal timing. I have a new idea for a book that I've been kicking around. But for some reason I haven't been able to get it off the ground. So I scrolled down to an arbitrary page of 100-WHATS of CREATIVITY.

I landed on What-If #32, "What if it was in the yearbook?" And by answering the questions on this page, I was immediately able to get a feel for the mood and attitude of my book, the audience for whom I am writing... and the way to present it!

This book is an amazing catalyst for getting unstuck, or for moving a project to the next step. I am now going to go open to another page and see what else I can discover about my new book.

I think what you've got is fantastic!
I will be reading it cover to cover.

I read these types of books that way once, just so I can store some of the ideas in my long-term memory and know where to go on my shelf for just such a resource.

The ideas also prompt me with exercises for my creative writing workshops by just reading straight through until something jumps up and hits me.

And then I follow the muse.

~ Bonnie Neubauer

Ms. Neubauer is the creator of StorySpinner, a creativity tool designed to generate millions of ideas and topics for writers, artists, actors, students, parents — everyone! www.storyspinner.com

Updated Foreword
by Jim Canterucci

Don "The Idea Guy" Snyder is brilliant! He has taken idea consulting to the highest level. I've told scores of people that if they don't have Don on retainer and on speed dial they are experiencing an unacceptable level of opportunity cost. As in, What if... you miss a multi-million dollar opportunity because you didn't enhance your idea by asking these great questions? Throughout these pages Don has provided a tool for your brain that you can really use. The What if... questions are extremely stimulating to brilliant idea generation. The quotes that set off the questions are truly words to live by for the innovator.

I've known Don personally and professionally for a few years now and I've always admired his ability to stand toe-to-toe during an intense 'beanstorm,' stretching from extremely complex to obviously simple, from loud and boisterous to quiet and thoughtful, and always from blank piece of paper to brilliant idea. I don't know anyone who uses the four catalysts of Personal Brilliance – Awareness, Curiosity, Focus, and Initiative more obviously than Don.

I have this book on my desk at all times, and in my computer too for any time I get stuck. My latest product idea is starting to take form. It's a monitoring tool – a boring looking piece of hardware and software, but it can save lives. *What-if #31.* What if... it was employed?, caused me to think of my device as an air traffic controller – very busy, diligently focused, prepared to leap into action at the first sign of trouble but doing it in a calm, assertive way. Wow, how different from a black box and jumble of wires.

Don't think this book is just creativity mumbo-jumbo though. There are some very practical questions you must ask yourself. Like #49. What if... the idea fails?

And, just as important, #50. What if... the idea succeeds?

Use this book. Carry it with you. Let the questions fuel your learning. Unleash your brilliance!

~ *Jim Canterucci*
Author of Personal Brilliance
www.mypersonalbrilliance.com

Introduction

When I originally assembled the 100-WHATS book back in 2001, I had no idea of the reception it would get from the small group of people with whom I shared it.

The small, self-published print run of 300 copies went much faster than I imagined, and the PDF ebook version continues to pop-up in the oddest of places: from recommended reading list for filmmakers attending The Ohio State University, to a bootleg translated version posted on an Israeli engineering website.

Most recently I was asked permission by Kraft Foods to allow distribution of a printable electronic version to their development team for use in the company's ideation process. How could I say 'no' to the creators of "Cheese and Macaroni?" This also means 100-WHATS will be translated into French for their offices in Canada.

Which brings us to this updated print version. And you.

A lot (most) of these questions may seem strange.

Good.

Creating a personality for your ideas by asking these 100-WHATS questions can go a long way toward helping in the development, marketing, and expansion of your original concept.

If you're wondering what kind of pizza your idea would eat (#43) — Your brain may unlock long enough to allow your thought process to move forward. Knowing that if your product breaks, the pieces can be turned into something else (#19), speaks to both the manufacturing process and the intended use of the product. Something your audience would definitely want to learn through your marketing message.

If you're working in a collaborative group, it is helpful to know how each team member would answer the questions. Have the group choose a series of question numbers and answer them from their individual point of view. Trade answer sheets. Do all your team members have the same concept of the idea in their minds — or is each working under a different set of assumptions about the idea's "personality?"

So, while some of these questions may cause you to smirk, chuckle, or roll your eyes — whenever you're stumped, or your mind is stuck in the muck — turn to one of these 100-WHAT questions and learn something new about your idea through your answers.

May all your ideas be BIG ideas...

PS: For bonus material, a free ebook version, and to submit your own 100-WHAT questions for inclusion in future editions, please visit www.100whatsbook.com

1. What If...

This is the single most important question in the creative process.

Without "What If" we wouldn't have — electric lights, indoor plumbing, the 10-speed bicycle, or even sent a man to the moon!

When we stop asking "What If" we are saying to the world, "There is no more room for improvement, everything is hunky-dory just as it is... we are content with the status quo."

Unfortunately, we would also be saying that creativity is dead. And if we submit to this premise, we may as well agree with the U.S. Patent Office when in 1899 they made the rumored statement, "Everything that can be invented already has been."

It is what we learn after we know it all that really counts.

2. What if...
It was bigger?

Not just a little bit bigger, but what if it was HUGE!

King Kong size!
Mickey D's Super-Sized
The Biggest Gulp

Perhaps calculators that you jump on like a trampoline to press the keys. Or a new design for a large floor lamp that is modeled after a mini book light. Crayons that you have to wrap both arms around. A computer mouse that you can get inside and drive (you'd push pedals to click the buttons.)

What's the BIGGEST you can imagine it?
Now, DOUBLE it in size.

"Did you know a lightning bug can only light-up when moving forward?

That's when we shine brightest too, when we take an idea and begin moving forward."

3. What if...
It was smaller?

Make dishes smaller to have portions appear larger. Smaller credit cards fit on your watchband for easy scanning.

Make skyscrapers smaller for interior decor (the Empire State Building in your living room!) Smaller office phones would take up less space on your desk

...Or what if pens were made smaller to better fit behind your ear?

4. What if...
It was thicker?

A highlighter that can cover an entire paragraph (or an entire page) in one swipe, tire rubber 10-inches thick, winter shirts that have a self-contained second layer...

How about a mattress that's thicker at the headboard to includes its own pillow area?

Kool-Aid that's more syrup than water?
Chewable applesauce?

Thicker baseball caps that offer increased head protection for little league players?

How can you improve your idea by making it thicker?

5. What if...
It was thinner?

A pen that folds flat into a notebook, computer cables on self-retracting spools to avoid the mess of wires behind your computer.

How about a radio so thin it fits in the back of your Daytimer — or in your business card case — or in the arm of your sunglasses? Perfect for the beach!

A TV remote control that is thin enough to be flexible, allowing it to wrap around the arm of your chair.

Thin items are easy to transport and store. You can carry more of them in your arms and are cheaper to ship because they weigh less and you can fit more in a single container.

How many ways can you think of to make your idea thinner?

6. What if...
It was taller?

A dinner table and chairs tall enough to swing your legs without touching the ground.

Stilt-Shoes you wear to clean gutters.

A bed tall enough to allow a chest of drawers to fit below.

What about doubling parking lot capacity by making some cars tall enough to park an additional car beneath?

What big benefits can you add to your idea by making it stand tall?

7. What if...
It was fatter?

A folding chair with a fat, padded seat.

Upholstery that gets fatter and overstuffed the more you use it.

Tires that have a canister of air built in to make flat tires fat tires.

Cups, cans and glassware so fat that they couldn't possibly spill over.

What if you sent direct mail advertisement out in envelopes that were padded — so that it seemed something important (or fragile) was contained inside? Do you think these "fatter envelopes" could increase your response rate?

8. What if...
It was wider?

Folding chairs wide enough for two people.

A toothbrush wide enough to clean your top and bottom teeth at the same time.

Pillows wide enough to cover the mattress edge to edge.

What if watchbands were wide enough to hold a calendar, a to-do list and one of those small pens from question #3?

Wider can mean additional comfort, spacious surroundings, or a larger viewing area on a TV screen.

What does wider mean to your idea?

9. What if...
It was slower?

Cars that automatically slow down in school zones.

A voice filter that slows down the speech of fast-talking salespeople.

Vitamins that slow the aging process.

What if you could make the evening hours go slower, lengthening your time away from work?

Developing computer programs more slowly could mean fewer bugs in the software, resulting in a stronger product.

How can being slower benefit your idea?

10. What if...
It smelled?

Sweaters that smell like coffee.
Scarves that smell like hot chocolate.
A watch that smells like vanilla.
Hiking boots with the aroma of freshly mown grass.

Our sense of smell affects how we perceive the world.

Think about a cottage hidden away in the snow covered mountains.

What do you smell?
The wood burning in the fireplace?
The smell of cinnamon and apples as the spiced cider warms on the stove?

What smell does your idea or product most represent?

"To create cool ideas you have to hang around cool people.

Magicians and madmen inspire creative thought, not pencil-pushers and bean-counters."

11. What if...
You could see it?

If you can see it in your mind, you can make it real.

Draw a picture of it, paint its portrait, mold it in clay, carve it in wood — create a prototype.

A three-dimensional prototype allows you to see your idea from all angles in real space.

Tower over it and look down on the prototype (they look like ants from up here). Set the model on a tabletop and lie on the floor and looking up at it (it's a bird, it's plane...!)

12. What if...
You could feel it?

Creating a three-dimensional prototype (#11) also allows you to actually touch your idea.

Hold it in your hands and press it against your flesh.

Is it hot? Cold? Sharp? Hard? Soft? Round? Wet? Bumpy? Slippery?

How will it feel when your customer holds it?

How will your customer feel?

13. What if...
It was flavored?

Okay, so maybe your product or idea isn't edible.

But is it in good or bad taste?

Will using your product leave a "bad taste" in someone's mouth? Or is the idea so good you can "taste" it?

The new iPod Shuffle is available in colors that look tasty. Even a recent mobile phone was available in a model called "Chocolate."

Can you add a flavor to your idea?

What If you made the ends of pens and pencils flavored — Lollipop Pens?

I've seen many people, deep in thought, chewing on writing instruments — They may as well taste good!

14. What if...
It made noise?

Shhh! Is your idea LOUD or quiet?

Does it jump out at you, demanding your attention? Or does it work in the background, so quiet and unassuming that you don't even know it's there?

Either option could be good (or bad) depending upon the type of project you're working.

A car radio that adjusts its volume according to the noise in and around the car would be very useful — People are forever turning the volume up and down.

Did you ever notice that people lower the volume of the radio when looking for a street address? It's almost as if a quiet radio improves their vision!

"Just because you own a small business doesn't mean you have to think small.

Think big to get bigger."

15. What if...
It was colorful?

Earth tones? Jewel tones? Pastels? Bold primary colors? Blinding fluorescent? The spectrum is endless, but every color affects how your idea will be received.

Some sales of the madly successful iPod can be attributed to its cute design and colorful cases. Have you noticed that almost EVERYONE designs their products to mimic the iPod colors?

Remember the iMac? I recall everything from trashcans to calculators molded in those oh-so popular translucent colors.

What color trend can you begin?
How about glow-in-the-dark?

Glow-in-the-dark house paint would make it easier to locate your house at night, but the market for that product is (probably) very small.

16. What if...
It had a texture?

Bumpy, bubbly, furry, curvy, cuddly, ridged, ribbed, waffled, sticky, slippery, sharp, silky, ???

Rough or smooth? Which is better for your idea?
Both work great as sandpaper.
Will both work great for your idea?

Silky sheets and fuzzy slippers are popular.
Ridges in a skillet make for a great indoor grill.

Can you make curvy computer disks?
A honeycombed bookcase?

What texture can you add to your idea to make it more useful or desirable?

17. What if...
It had a pattern?

Is every third widget blue?

Do your customers purchase an entire set to create an image out of the packages? Video collections sometimes take advantage of this type of design.

Does it come in herringbone or tweed, like a sports coat? (A herringbone TV? A tweed toaster?)

Does it have lines, polka dots, zigzag, waves, flecks, checkers, ink spots, thumbprints, boxes, bows, flowers...?

18. What if...
You asked a Fool?

In medieval times the Fool was the only person allowed to poke fun at the King's law.

Through his jesting he influenced the King's opinion, allowing the King to see the "other side" of ideas and concepts.

What fools can you hang around with?

Encourage silly ideas.

When I get together to brainstorm, my ears prick up whenever someone prefaces their idea with "This might sound cheesy, but..."

Behold! The Power of Cheese.

"If too many people like your idea, you're not thinking big enough."

Don!

19. What if...
It was broken?

Would it be fatal?

Would it still work?

Would you have twice as many?

Must you break it in order to use it?

Kit Kat candy bars are made to break into five pieces.

There was an early coin minted in the shape of a clover. To spend it, you broke off the "leaves" and used them as smaller denominations.

How would the United States dollar look if you could break it into quarters? What if you could break a five-dollar bill into ones?

Would it look like a Kit Kat?

20. What if...
It was a Super Hero?

All Lois Lane had to do was scream Superman's name and he would fly to her rescue.

What do your customers need to do in order to have your product or service "rescue" them?

A computer back-up program has the power to turn back time. Krazy Glue has super strength. FedEx delivers packages at super speed.

Superman could fly, had super strength, leap tall buildings in a single bound, yadda, yadda, yadda...

What powers does your idea have?

21. What if...
It was an animal?

What animal best represents your idea?

Sly like a fox?

Wise like an owl?

Strong like a bull?

Are the qualities of the "animal" (the American Indians used guiding animal spirits called "totems") reflected in your finished product? (A lion's mane, the sleekness of a race horse, etc.)

A gas station formerly used the phrase "Put a tiger in your tank."

What animal can you put in your product?

22. What if...
It came from another culture?

Is it fragile like a Ming vase?

Foggy like England?

Gourmet like France?

Frozen like Antarctica?

In the shape of a boot like Italy?

Companies sell English breakfast tea. Irish pubs are popular places to meet.

There are plenty of steakhouses that call upon the spirit of Texas.

What geographical or cultural attributes can you graft onto your idea?

"Want bigger and better ideas?

Get larger groups of people together for brainstorming sessions.

Bigger Groups = Bigger Ideas."

23. What if...
It came from another planet?

Is your idea "of this world?"

Is it a hero from Krypton, like Superman, or an evil invader from Mars?

Does it appear out of nowhere? (Beam me up, Scotty!)
Does it move at warp speed?
Phasers on stun?

Does the package look like a flying saucer?
Is it "serialized" like the old Flash Gordon movies?

What interplanetary ideas can be added to your product?

24. What if...
It's a Pisces?

As hokey as it may seem, people born under specific astrological signs possess certain characteristics.

Horoscope signs represent Fire, Water, Air, and Earth. Hot tempered, creative, patient, honest... All these are said to be influenced by the signs under which we are born.

What is the astrological sign for your idea?

When was it "born"?

Read the daily horoscope for your idea.

25. What if...
It was a candy bar?

Is it like a Milky Way, with a gooey center?

Nutty, like a PayDay?

Classic, like a Hershey bar?

Thick like a Chunky bar?

Compact like M&Ms?

Sweet like a Hershey's Kiss?

Sour like a Skittles?

Hot like a Fireball?

What makes your idea a treat to use?

26. What if...
It was a season?

Colorful, crunchy, and crisp like Autumn?
Bright, new and green like Spring?
Hot, sandy and sunny like Summer?
White, pure and cold like Winter?

How can your idea instill feelings of a particular season all year round?

Dryer sheets smell springtime fresh.
Lemonade tastes like summer.

What season is most like your idea?

"An idea that's bold is worthless until sold!"

27. What if...
It had a name?

If our ideas are like our children — we've got to name them, don't we?

A name can hold power.

Get a book of baby names with meanings and christen your idea.

Can your idea live up to the name it's been bestowed?

Ferrari, Edison, Disney, Lincoln, Napoleon...

Or will it be an Edsel?

28. What if...
It had an apartment?

Does it keep the house neat as a pin,
or is there dirty laundry everywhere?

An expensive penthouse or a tiny hole in the wall?

Lots of family pictures on the walls?
A monster stereo system?
Does your idea play video games?

A kitchen a chef would be proud of,
or a countertop covered in take-out menus?

What personality does your idea display in its habitat?

29. What if...
It had a hobby?

Does your idea play on a softball league?

Drive a racecar?

Collect stamps?

Paint portraits?

Trade sports cards, collect comic books, wine tasting, bowling, ballroom dancing?

Hobbies add interest to a person's life, how can they make your idea more interesting?

30. What if...
It was an automobile?

A big gas-guzzler or an economy car?

A convertible sports car or the family stationwagon?

American-made, or an import?

Candy-apple red or metallic gray?

A dragster or a bumper-car?

What does your idea look like when transformed into an automobile?

"Thinking creative thoughts and behaving creatively can get you called a 'Meathead.'

Can you take it?"

31. What if...
It was employed?

Your idea can't just have any job, right?

Does your idea lust after the big, corner office with the window? Or does it already sit in the big office, with its legs up on the desk perusing the latest copy of the Wall Street Journal?

Does your idea show up for work everyday in a sleeveless t-shirt, wearing a hardhat?

Maybe it's an idea working its way through college, delivering pizzas.

Or does your idea ask the eternal question — "Ya want fries with that?"

32. What if...
It was in the yearbook?

Did your idea graduate from an Ivy League school, or did it learn its lessons on the streets in the school of hard knocks?

What kind of grades did it get?
Did it do its homework?

Was it in the drama club?
Track team?
Chess club?

Which clique did your idea hang out with — the Brains, the Brawn or the Beautiful people?

33. What if...
It had an attitude?

It's been said, "Attitude is a small thing that makes a big difference."

What difference would a strong attitude make to your idea's profile?

There used to be a battery commercial that demonstrated a "tough guy" attitude when it dared viewers to knock a battery off the shoulder of its spokesperson.

Is your idea tough?
Happy?
Grouchy?
Sarcastic?

If your idea could speak to you, what tone of voice would it use?

34. What if...
It played a sport?

Is your idea the Michael Jordan of concepts?

A baseball star?
Football hero?

Maybe it plays golf?
Hockey?

Does it glide like a downhill skier, float like a hang-glider, or fly through the air like a pole-vaulter?

Will your idea qualify for the next Olympics?
If it did, will it win the gold, silver or bronze medal?
In which event?

35. What if...
It had a favorite food?

Spicy Mexican burritos, or over-priced nouveau cuisine?

Does it eat in a nice sit-down restaurant, a street cafe, or does your idea just hit the drive-thru?

Plenty of fiber in your idea's diet?

Perhaps your idea is a vegetarian?

What if your idea only worked in conjunction with vegetables (food processor)... Or made hamburgers easier? (The George Foreman grill.)

What foods appeal to your idea?

36. What if...
It watched movies?

Does your idea like scary movies?
Classic films?
Science Fiction?
Westerns?

How about different flavored popcorn for different movie genres? (Cheddar for "cheesy" B-movies, Caramel for sweet love stories, etc.)

A great movie idea in the fifties was something called the "Tingler", it caused the seats to vibrate during especially shocking scenes in the movie. The promoter made audience members sign a waiver releasing the theater from liability if they were "scared to death."

Brilliant!
If you're a fan of horror movies how could you NOT go see a movie that was so scary you were required to sign a legal document?

37. What if...
It was a movie character?

As longs as we're on the topic of movies...
Is your idea more of a Dirty Harry or a Mary Poppins?

Will your concept be so ingenious it'll "make your day" or will you need a "spoonful of sugar" to make it go down?

Is it a young idea making its way in the world like Luke Skywalker, or a seasoned adventurer on a quest like Indiana Jones?

Most movie characters are archetypal personalities. Which archetype does your idea most resemble?

Hero?
Villain?
Mentor?
Best friend?

38. What if...
It listens to music?

Yo, dude! We're rockin' out to some awesome ideas!

Listening to country, rock, punk, classical, jazz, blues, funk, even disco music* can affect your creativity. You can even channel your creative styles based on the genre of music you're listening to at any given time.

Try listening to different types of music and watch your creativity jam!

*WARNING: If disco is involved, the results could be frightening!

"You have to feed your brain a steady diet of new experiences if you want it to grow up big and strong and bright.

It takes the right kind of brain food to fuel creative thinking."

39. What if...
It was like a TV program?

Your ideas would be very different if they went from watching a political program to watching a comedy.

Well, maybe not that different...

Which TV show is your idea most like?
Edgy and dramatic like The Shield?
Quirky and unusual like Seinfeld?
Ironic and spooky like the Twilight Zone?

Is it "Must See TV" or something about to get cancelled?

Is your idea more like an after-school special,
or a prime time mini-series?

40. What if...
It drinks?

Are we talking pulp-novel, liver-rotting, whiskey-swilling, detective-style drinking?

Maybe the idea is a teetotaler — sticking to non-alcoholic beverages like Kool-Aid or soda pop?

Perhaps your idea is more of a good old boy named "Bubba" sipping some corn-squeezings on his front porch. What if the concept is more of a secret drinker, hiding a bottle in the bottom drawer of its desk — sipping shots when no one is looking, afraid of being discovered?

Maybe it's strictly a social drinker, meeting its friends for the occasional happy hour. Lots of laughs and nursing a hangover the next day.

41. What if...
It has a bedtime?

Does your idea doze off in the armchair before Wheel of Fortune is over, or does it stay up late channel surfing throughout the night?

Does your idea or product have specific hours of operation and use, or does it go on forever — a true 24/7/365 concept?

Perhaps your idea needs a glass of water before it's tucked in at night.

What kind of sheets does it sleep on?
Is the bed a bunk bed, waterbed, or does it fall asleep on the couch?

42. What if...
It was edible?

A steak and potatoes type of idea — performing to
perfection only the most basic of functions — or are we
talking about the haute cuisine of concepts where style
rules the plate?

Paper or cloth napkins?

Is your idea similar to a street vendor hawking hot dogs
or closer to some high-falutin' joint where you bribe the
maitre de just to get your name on a six-month waiting
list for reservations?

There's a taste for every palate — what's yours?

"Creative thinkers should draw and paint and doodle and sculpt and weld and build and mold and cut and paste and glue and tear and staple and sing and dance and mime and act — creating physical manifestations of their idea.

Some ideas cannot be expressed by words alone."

43. What if...
It orders pizza?

What would the pizza guy deliver?

Cheese only?
Pepperoni? Sausage?
The "Works?"

Would the idea be sucking down anchovies — or would it be some fancy-schmancy wood-fired specialty pizza with imported duck-sausage and portabello mushrooms?

Ordered from a large franchise, a neighborhood joint, or did you knead the dough with your own two hands?

Thick or thin crust?
Hand-tossed or deep dish?

How would it tip the delivery guy?

44. What if...
Its friends visited?

Would you like the crowd your "child" was hanging out with?
Leather-jacketed hoodlums — or chess-club geeks?

Are they throwing pajama parties on the weekend or breaking into your liquor cabinet while you're asleep?

Who your idea hangs out with reflects on your concept. What other related products are in your field?

Do you want your "baby" to be associated with them? If you had a choice, what associations would you arrange?

45. What if...
You bought it a present?

Would your idea be unwrapping socks and underwear?
A polka dot tie?
Maybe Santa brought a bicycle?

Which gifts would your idea enjoy?

Which gifts would it hate?

What toys would your idea play with?

"Ideas are gifts from
the devil.

The greater the idea — the more
passionate you are about the
concept — the better the chance
you'll go mad trying to bring it into
reality."

46. What if...
It likes poetry?

Frost?
Browning?
Byron?
Keats?
Tupac?

Whose voice speaks to the spirit of your idea?
What words ring true to its heart?

Does your idea walk in beauty like the night, or does it take the road less traveled?

What creative words inspire your creativity?

47. What if...
It has a favorite book?

Does your idea delve into the dark world of Sylvia Plath?
The fantasy of Tolkein?
The humor and wit of Twain?

Do you read it a bedtime story from the Brothers
Grimm, or does your idea read romance novels while
enjoying a hot bubble bath?

Does it read the latest best seller, or thumb through
used paperbacks?

What if your idea WAS a book?
Who would be the author?

48. What if...
It wore clothes?

Jeans and t-shirt or Brookes Brothers suit?
Sunday morning church clothes or an eternal casual day at the office?

Air Jordan or Gucci on its feet?

Does it wear a top hat and tails like Fred Astaire or a baseball cap and drooping overalls like Dennis The Menace?

Tailor-made or off the rack?

When you create supplemental product for your idea, will they have to be custom made, or will one size fit all?

49. What if...
The idea fails?

Would you start again or close up shop and go into another business?
Would you build on the existing concept or abandon it all together to pursue a completely new idea?

What does a failure say about the market for your product?
The project execution?
The personnel involved?

What will you have learned?
What lessons can you take to the next project?

What constitutes a failure?

"Ideas popping into your head in the middle of the night always turn out to be the brightest.

...And the hardest to decipher when you wake in the morning."

50. What if...
The idea succeeds?

Retirement in the Bahamas?
Constant improvements and upgrades to the idea?
Buy up smaller support companies?
Sell the finished concept to a mega-company?

Will there be imitators?
How difficult (or easy) is it to duplicate?
What will they change to make their knock-off more successful than your original?

What will you have learned?
What lessons can you take to the next project?

What constitutes a success?

51. What if...
You're scared?

Are you afraid of failure?
Afraid of success?
...of appearing foolish?

Sometimes thinking seriously about what you fear most can put you back on the right track.

Once you expose your fears to the light of day and literally speak them aloud, they no longer appear so dark and foreboding.

If you're afraid of what people might say behind your back, remember that Oscar Wilde said the only thing worse than being talked about is NOT being talked about.

52. What if...
You are certain?

Instead of dwelling on the unknown, why not review the "known?"

Is there a need for your product?

Do you know your manufacturing costs?

The time needed to put your concept into action?

Required resources?

Every project needs a progress checklist, keep your morale high by creating a list of "positive project certainties."

53. What if...
There are risks?

Don't be ignorant of (or hide from) the true risks.

Knowing what the dangers are ahead of time can allow you to minimize (or completely avoid) anticipated pitfalls and challenges.

If you're planning a trip and you know there is construction on the originally selected travel path, wouldn't you plot an alternate course (or at least anticipate a delay in reaching your destination?)

Looking at the downside doesn't necessarily make you a pessimist —
it makes you prepared.

54. What if...
There are rewards?

Okay, you looked at the downside — now what's the upside?

Constantly fantasizing about the "great things" that will happen to you when you strike it rich can be hazardous to your idea.

BUT, reviewing why you're doing all this in the first place can keep you motivated when the chips are down.

It's okay to daydream. It's alright to visit fantasyland. Just don't move there full-time.

"If you have an idea that will help someone else, share it with them.

You never know when they may have an idea for you."

55. What if...
You focus on the problem?

Take another look at what prompted you to start this train of thought.

Once you've traveled down a single track to a solution, it's easy to lose sight of the problem that started it all.

Is the idea you're working on going to solve your original problem?

It's perfectly acceptable to make course adjustments.

56. What if...
You solve more than one problem?

Sure, you probably started out working on ONE solution, but what about all the other ideas that you're not working on?

I find it's always helpful to have two, three, or even five projects in process at one time. The best ideas usually come to me when I'm working on something else.

You've probably come up with great ideas while you were in the shower or driving to work. That's because setting your conscious mind on an alternate task allows your subconscious to solve the big problems that are "really" bugging you!

57. What if...
You had to defend your idea?

Are you willing to stand up for your concept?
Willing to fight for it?

Die for it?

How much are you dedicated to the idea as it currently
exists?
Are you willing to negotiate changes?

Does the success of the idea depend on keeping its
original integrity intact?

58. What if...
It could do something different?

Can your idea multi-task?
A lot of products serve more than one purpose.

Does yours?

If your idea only does one thing, can you make it do another? If it already does two things, can you make it do three?

Four?

"No matter how advanced computers get, or how intuitive graphics programs become —

Nothing beats sketching out an idea on the back of a cocktail napkin."

59. What if...
You were in the IDEAL situation?

If you've ever used a pencil to trace your way through a maze drawn on paper, you may have found it's easier to solve the maze by starting at the end and working your way backward to the start.

What is the ideal conclusion to your project?
Patent? Trademark?
Fame? Fortune?

All of the above?
Something completely different?

Think about exactly what you want.
Put it in writing.

Now work your way backward — what path do you need to follow in order to end up at your final (ideal) destination?

60. What if...
You had the WORST solution?

What IS the worst solution?
Could it be turned around and made better?

How did you arrive at the worst solution?

Could the problem be reframed to make your solution
more compatible?

Does your "worst" solution solve another problem you
hadn't yet considered — or even knew was an issue?

61. What if...
You made a commercial?

What benefits would you advertise to consumers?

What guarantees?

Who would be your spokesperson?

During what program would your commercial air?

What imagery would appear in your commercial?
Animated or live action?
Special effects?

What's your favorite commercial?
Would it still be your favorite if it advertised your idea?
What changes would you make?

62. What if...
Your idea had a theme song?

From Barney the Dinosaur's "I Love You, You Love Me" to McDonald's "You Deserve a Break Today" to the Gilligan's Island theme song — Jingles invade your brain and lodge themselves into your gray matter.

What does your idea have that's worth singing about?

Who would do the singing?

Sinatra?
A church choir?
Adam Sandler?

63. What if...
You surrendered your idea?

What if you gave it up?
Just chucked the whole thing and started from scratch?

Would you relish the newly found freedom from your previous chains of commitment?

Consider burning your existing "mental map" and charting a completely new course of creativity.

"There's always a better way to do something.

There is a creative genius in every frustrated individual who's dissatisfied with the way things currently exist."

64. What if...
You asked someone else's opinion?

Additional insight can be helpful, especially when you're at a dead-end. But, it must be welcomed with open arms.

Don't make excuses —
"I was gonna do that."
"I tried it that way."
"I would have done that, but..."

Say these things in your head (if you must) but not to the person sharing their opinion with you.

Their initial comments may seem simple to you (you already tried something, or considered that particular option) but they need to work their way past the obvious options before they can get to the good-stuff you might consider useful.

65. What if...
You looked at it sideways?

You know how you'll sometimes catch a glimpse of something out of the corner of your eye?

Why not catch an inspiration or an insight?

Close your eyes.
Think about your situation for a few seconds.

Now, slowly rotate your head sideways and rest it on your shoulder. If you created a prototype (#11) or have some item that provides a visual cue to your problem — face the item and open your eyes.

What does your new perspective reveal to you?

What if you stood on your head?

66. What if...
You combined it with something?

Great stuff can come from combining two (or more) different ideas.

The first thing that comes to mind is Reese's Cups! Peanut butter and chocolate... Mmm!

Combining two items can make them twice as useful.
Lamp + Portability = Flashlight
Lamp + Portability + Hands-Free = Headlamp

What if coffee beans could be purchased in a combination disposable grinder, brewer and cup?

What can you partner with your idea to make it more useful...
More Successful?
More Popular?
More Valuable?

67. What if...
You made it simpler?

Most things can be simplified.

Think in terms of a first-time user.
Will a person seeing your idea for the first time
understand how it works?

Does it require elaborate instructions or training?
What can you do to streamline its use?

All things being equal — wouldn't you buy a product
that's easy to use?
Wouldn't everyone?

"Make lists of items and then combine them in a unique way.

The PalmPilot was basically a combination of a pocket calculator and a notepad.

The iPod is basically a PalmPilot and a Walkman."

68. What if...
You made it difficult?

Difficult doesn't have to mean "bad."

Perhaps your product is more advanced than others in the market are, users may require special certification before beginning its use, and perhaps your product has additional features that others do not.

A product perceived as more difficult could also be perceived as more valuable. More hoops to jump through could translate as a more "high-tech" solution; A more advanced product requiring more educated users.

What can you do to increase the value of your product through the introduction of user-hurdles?

69. What if...
You force it?

Can't make it fit?
Force it!

Kids are great at this.

They'll twist toys every which way while playing, and if they break it...
They'll play with the pieces.

What if you force your round project into a square hole?

What if you force it into a more convenient shape?
A better container?

What pieces can you play with?

Use (the) Force, Luke!

70. What if...
You shift direction?

Just a small change can make a huge difference.

The tiniest shift in the course of a meteor in space can cause it to come crashing into the Earth. (Or so the movies say.)

Just a few degrees can mean the difference between life and death.

What can you shift on your project?

Shift changes and their effects can be cumulative — A tiny shift now could mean dramatic changes down the road.

A directional shift can mean the difference between finding a shorter route to the West Indies and discovering a whole New World.

Find out where you'd like to be, and start making small shifts in your course to get there.

71. What if...
You rearrange it?

Think rearranging stuff doesn't mean much?

You may have heard the saying "You're just rearranging deck chairs on the Titanic." Meaning, the situation is already doomed, why bother?
This is not always the case.

As it exists, the alphabet doesn't actually spell anything, but rearranging the letters creates our entire written language.

A simple rearrangement of a finite number of letters allows for the creation of our greatest written works.

Shakespeare had no more letters to create with than you did, he just put them in the right order to create his place in history.

What can you rearrange to leave your mark?

72. What if...
You just relax?

Stressed?
Stumped?
Is your brain locked?

Take a break.

Listen to music.
Read a book.
See a movie.
Grab something to eat.

Just walk away from the problem for an hour or two.

The world won't come to an end, and you won't need to buy a toupee because you pulled all your hair out in frustration!

73. What if...
You rotate it?

A twist to the left opens most bottles and jars.

Twisting a screw to the right enables you to lock two pieces of wood together to form building frames.

Rotating the tires on your automobile can extend their life, saving you money.

Can you rotate something on your idea to save your customer time or money?

Perhaps it's the location of your control buttons, or where the power source is located. Maybe it's as ridiculously simple as turning it completely upside down...

Hey, it works for the Magic 8-Ball!

"If you're unable to put a great idea into action —
Give it to someone who can.

There is nothing more worthless than a notebook full of ideas that could have changed the world."

74. What if...
You ask an Oracle?

When the ancient Greeks needed guidance, they asked the gods. Oracles provided a voice to the gods. They were wise beyond measure and answered (most times cryptically) the questions brought before them.

The trick to using a modern Oracle is seeking a source that WON'T give you a straight answer!

Form a question regarding your project.
Make it specific. Write it down. Consult your chosen Oracle.

Read your horoscope. Use tarot cards.
Choose random words out of a book.
Use a line from a movie, song, or poem.

Use this offbeat and unrelated information to plan your next move.

75. What if...
You beat it with a hammer?

Seems like a pretty simple question, doesn't it?
If you hit it with a hammer it'll break!

Right?
Not necessarily...

You could dent it, scuff it, shatter it, chip it, knock a hole in it, the hammer could bounce off, it could make a sound like a drum or a cymbal or chimes, or a gong, it could strike sparks, set off an explosion — or the hammer could even break!

What else can you hit it with...?

76. What if...
It bounced?

If you hurtled your idea to the hard ground...
would it bounce?

Would it simply return to your hands, or would it double
its height like a "Super Ball?"

You don't have to take this question literally. Think of
bouncing as how your product responds to setbacks.
If you encounter a problem, will it "bounce" back?

Will its success bounce you into a new tax bracket?
Will its failure bounce you out on your behind?

77. What if...
A child invented it?

Large, colorful controls?
Simple and easy to use?
More durable and long lasting?

Perhaps it makes funny noises when you push control buttons.

Maybe there are pictures of cartoon characters.

Users may consider it fun to use instead considering it work. It's viewed as game play instead of laborious chores.

Using it could bring a smile to your customer's face.

78. What if...
You wrote a joke about it?

The funniest (meaning most successful) comedians appeal to their audiences by pointing out the humorous side of everyday life.

Things that are "too true."

Even if the comedian's material speaks of inequality, racism, and other serious topics concerning our society — their humor points out the common plight, making everyone acknowledge (between the giggles and guffaws) that there IS a problem.

What serious truths can you find in your project to poke fun at? What troubles can you make light of?

Find solutions within your laughter.

79. What if...
You slept on it?

Does your brain hurt from thinking about your project too much?

Then there's only one thing to do... Take a nap.

That's right.
Catch some Zs, visit dreamland, call the Sandman — just go to bed.

Close your eyes and let your mind catch some insight from your subconscious.

Thomas Edison didn't really sleep what anyone might consider a "normal" night's rest. Instead, he took small naps throughout the day. He even had a sleep station in his lab to catch a few Zs whenever the mood struck him.

A new way to look at your problem —
Through your eyelids!

"A *good* idea solves problems.

A *great* idea solves
problems at a profit."

80. What if...
It was someone else's problem?

Can't find a solution to your situation... Give it away!

Hand off your problem to Einstein.
Or Copernicus. Edison. Franklin. Any expert you like.

View your puzzle from their perspective.

You don't need to be an expert on anyone else's life —
you just need to know the basic principles for which they
stood. It can be as easy as using a book of quotations.

Decide upon an individual whose input you'd appreciate
and find quotes from that person. Then, apply the
quotes to your specific situation.

I like to enlist Sherlock Holmes or even Batman to help
solve my problems. You can easily put them on the case
by renting a few titles from your friendly neighborhood
video store.

81. What if...
You met the next generation?

Stumped on where to go next with your idea?
Try to see the next version!

What are the logical advances to your idea or product?
In your competitor's product?

By looking into the near future (one or two years down
the road) you can work backwards to the successful
completion of the first version.

Peeking into the future can be quite an advantage!

82. What if...
You knew what your customers liked?

Knowing exactly what customers love (or hate!) about your product would be great, but you're not much of a mind reader, right?

Sit down and review each feature/benefit of your idea.

Pick out five things you like best.
Pick the five things you like least.

Now switch personalities.
Become your ideal customer — the one for which you can do no wrong — and work your way through the two lists again. You'll collect glowing praise in this mindset, even the "bad stuff" doesn't seem so horrible.

Now try it again.
This time as the cranky old man down the street.
He hates everything.

How does he feel about your idea?
What can you do to improve his opinion?

83. What if...
It was made of gold?

Aside from the obvious (melt it down and cash it in!)
What else would making the product out of precious
materials mean?

Would it increase the functional value of your project? In
the past, gold was considered the best material for filling
cavities in teeth.

Or could making it out of gold (or diamonds, or silver, or
rubies) actually decrease its real-world value and
usefulness? Using a soft metal like gold to make the
head of a hammer would create one heck of a useless
(but very expensive!) hammer.

Strive to make your idea so useful, so functional, so
revolutionary — that even if you made it out of platinum
it wouldn't increase the value of its functional use to
your customers.

84. What if...
You were stranded with it?

Could it save your life?
Keep you from being bored?
Would it give you something to work on in your spare time?

If you knew you would be alone on an island with your idea — would you make any changes to it?
Would you want to be stranded with it?

What could you change to make your project indispensable in any situation? Create the Swiss Army Knife of ideas.

85. What if...
It existed in the distant past?

WOW!
Your idea — alive 1,000 years in the past.
It must've been revolutionary!

The simplest idea of our time existing in the past could
have changed the world.
Machine guns in the Revolutionary War...
Space travel during the middle ages...
Photography in the Jurassic period...

What would the world have thought of your idea so
many years ago?

"Creativity is a simple process. Unless you don't understand it.

Then, it's like trying to figure out a magic trick — a simple process for the magician, but a source of astonishment for the audience."

86. What if...
It existed in the future?

How would your concept be received if thrust 1,000 years into the future?

Would it still be revolutionary?
Or would the old-fashioned concept likely be met with a polite snicker?

Is it outdated — or still innovative?

What can you do to ensure your idea's originality into the far-flung future?

87. What if...
It was like Play-Doh?

What can you do to make your idea "squishy?"

Play-Doh has captured the attention of the public for years. It's malleable enough to take any shape and novel enough to make us smile.

It's a simple product in simple packaging.
It's reusable, economically replaceable, and its name says what it is.

How does your idea compare?

88. What if...
It was a Dr. Seuss character?

If your project walked on the beach,
like a Star-Bellied Sneech,
Would it put fame and fortune within your reach?

What learning could you learn,
Your brain filling up like a balloon,
if your idea was like a Dr. Seuss cartoon?

Imagine that — What would you do with powers like the
Cat in the Hat?
Would you invent the next Wicked Wonkster or make a
big wet Kersplat?

Would you package your idea in a box?
With an animal logo, like a fox?

Could your idea be a really big, super-duper deal?
Oh, what can you do to make your really big idea, really
really real?

89. What if...
You changed its use?

You started down your creative path by finding a problem and attempting to solve it. But, now you're stuck.

You've innovated yourself right into a corner. The idea has had unexpected results, and you don't know what to do.

How about this?
Find a different problem to solve.

Many great ideas came about by changing the problem it was intended to solve.

Name one, you say?
I'll name two.

Silly Putty and Post It Notes.

If you can't find an existing market for your project — invent your own!

90. What if...
Money was no object?

Unlimited funds to develop your project?
What would you do with all that money?

Make a list — All the things you would do if you had a
blank check to develop your idea. Now review your list
and come up with real-world alternatives that fall within
your budget.

Going to spend money on test marketing?
Hand out samples to your family.

Going to host a focus group?
Treat your coworkers to free pizza if they'll agree to use
your product and share their opinions afterward.

Big money doesn't always solve problems.
The creativity to produce your idea with limited funds
will keep you focused on your goal (the idea) instead of
the money.

91. What if...
It doesn't inspire you?

If your project doesn't inspire you, there are only two things you can do. Reframe the project in terms that do inspire you, or drop it and move on.

That's right.
Move on.

Life is too short to spend on projects that you're not excited about.
Find a project that moves you or move on.

"Brainstorms can flood
you with ideas.

You can gauge how successful a
brainstorming session was by how
bad your writer's cramp is
afterward.

Clock your creativity.
How many ideas did you generate
per hour?

How many per minute?"

92. What if...
You played with someone else's toys?

Did you know the playful Yo-Yo was originally a weapon?

The original Yo-Yo (yes, it had the same name) was a four-pound rock at the end of a 20-foot cord. It was used in two ways — the first was for hunting, the second was to fight off enemies.

It wasn't until 1927 when Donald Duncan first saw the Yo-Yo and turned it into the one of the best selling toys of all time.

What toys can you play with?
How can you re-purpose it's original use in order to create a brand new idea for a product?

93. What if...
An evil genius plots against your idea?

Villains plot against you — keeping your idea from being successful.

Put yourself in the role of the evil genius.
What schemes would you-as-the-Villain hatch to keep you-as-the-Innovator's ideas from becoming successful?

Write all your maniacal plans down (or have an evil henchman take notes for you.)

Okay — Snap out of it!
Back into your real role of the Innovative-Hero. Your job is to now come up with ways to defeat each one of the Evil Genius' plans.

By creating solutions to the evil plans, you'll be creating solutions to most of the real problems that will cross your path on the way to success.

94. What if...
Your idea evoked emotions?

Does your idea tug at the heartstrings or does it evoke insane jealousy?

Are you giggling with glee or sobbingly sorrowful?

Does it spark passionate loyalty or instill feelings of dull indifference?

If you're not satisfied after analyzing the feelings your product currently evokes, change your idea in order to provoke the response you desire.

Keep making adjustments until you feel good about the feelings your idea is spreading around.

95. What if...
Your competitor created it?

Your competitor just put an identical product on the market before you've even decided on your packaging. What are you going to do?

What (if any) changes will you make to your product before it hits the streets? Will you shelve your product, feeling you've been beaten to the punch? Will you delay your release until you can add new features?

Perhaps you'll choose to release your version as-is, getting it to market as quickly as possible in order to cash in on the excitement your competitor's product may generate.

What other choices can you think of?
What are benefits and faults in each of the options?

Why wait for threat of a competitor's product to force you to improve?
Do it now!

96. What if...
It was the opposite?

The world has started spinning backward!
Left is right, up is down, right is wrong, and innovative is boring.

Your product idea has just been transformed into its exact opposite.
What do you do?

A minor change to your advertising campaign, or a complete redesign of the product?

Has the problem you've been trying to solve also been reversed?

Has its solution been reversed as well?

"A creative person needs
to love selling.

It's not so much a sales
pitch as an exchange of excitement.

The thinker must transfer a portion
of their love for the idea to the
person who can put it into action."

97. What if...
It could move?

If your idea were imbued with the power of movement, what form would it take?

Crawl, walk, stroll, canter, gallop, skip, run, swing, saunter, limp, roll, jump, hop, fly, float, bounce, trot, plod, swim, burrow, etc.?

Or, take another approach... How will you move your product from one place to another?

Messenger, ship, plane, bicycle, automobile, truck, unicycle, fighter plane, speedboat, slingshot, pogo stick, parachute, street vendor, singing telegram...?

Perhaps your idea is SO cool it takes a limousine.

98. What if...
It was adjustable?

One size fits all. This usually (with the exception of some baseball hats) does not hold true.

Adjustable means you can personally make the necessary changes to have the item fit your needs. Adjustable chairs, desks, hats, car seats, etc.

What options on your idea can be made adjustable for the user?
Color cases for desktop computers?
Photo inserts for watches?

How can you apply adjustable options to your idea?

99. What if...
It came with accessories?

If you've ever heard anyone speak about fashion, one of the most common cliches is "accessorizing is everything."

Add a scarf, different jewelry, a belt, a hat, etc. and it's like getting several different outfits by spending a little more on accessories.

What items can you create for your product that will enhance its value through available accessories?

This is a way to make additional profits as well. Think about all the clothes and play-sets they sell for Barbie and Bratz dolls! How about all those extra items and add-ons for your iPod?

What pre-existing products are already on the market for which you could create a separate line of accessories?

100. What if...
You gave it to your grandmother?

Finally, what would your grandmother say if you gave her a copy of your concept, idea or product?

Would she be proud?
Excited?
Embarrassed?

My hope is that she would be proud of you.

When the world shares their opinion of your idea (and they will) just think about what your grandmother would say.

If you're true to your idea (and your ideals) — and it would make your grandmother proud — let the rest of the world have their own opinions. You'll have the only one that really matters.

Let them worry about what <u>their</u> grandmothers will say!

"The only thing more important than asking WHY, is asking... WHAT-IF?"

Don!

I hope you enjoyed
100-WHATS of CREATIVITY

I encourage you to keep this book on hand and refer to it whenever you stumble across a mental block. Consider these questions idea detours that will help you find your way back to the path of innovation.

I'd love to hear from anyone who has used 100-Whats to improve their creative process. Use the email address below, and send me stories of how you've put the power of 100-Whats to use.

Keep Thinking BIG,
~ Don The Idea Guy

What if...
You knew more about
the author?

Possessing creative powers beyond those of mere mortals, DON THE IDEA GUY rescues those in need of innovative ideas through his brainstorming sessions, seminars, articles, and website (www.dontheideaguy.com).

DTIG has sold, shared, or traded ideas with the likes of Sears-Kenmore, Ford Motor Company, Palm, American Airlines, Coca-Cola, Kelloggs, The American Marketing Association, Seth Godin, Daniel Pink, Jeffrey Gitomer, and The Tom Peters Company.

Don has written hundreds of articles on the topic of increasing business innovation and personal creativity. He's received coverage in notable publications like Small Business News, The New York Times, Fast Company, Forbes, and FORTUNE. He's also the author of "Boring Meetings Suck" (www.boringmeetingssuck.com).

Don The Idea Guy is an accomplished public speaker, an official "Trained Brain" of Doug Hall's Eureka Ranch, and served as the first president of the International Idea Trade Association.

What if...
You asked Don to increase YOUR creativity?

With a variety of individual and corporate programs that can be customized to your needs, Don The Idea Guy adds the differentiating factor of creativity to increase the innovation quotient in your personal and professional life.

Contact him today to begin turning all of your ideas into BIG ideas.

CONTACT:
Don The Idea Guy
PO Box 26392
Columbus, OH 43226
USA

(614) 340-7910 phone/fax

me@dontheideaguy.com
www.DonTheIdeaGuy.com